THE CLOUD VERSUS
GRAND UNIFICATION THEORY

CHRIS BANKS

ECW Press \ a misFit book

Copyright © Chris Banks, 2017

Published by ECW Press
665 Gerrard Street East, Toronto, ON M4M 1Y2
416-694-3348 / info@ecwpress.com

All rights reserved. No part of this publication may be reproduced, stored in a retrieval system, or transmitted in any form by any process — electronic, mechanical, photocopying, recording, or otherwise — without the prior written permission of the copyright owners and ECW Press. The scanning, uploading, and distribution of this book via the Internet or via any other means without the permission of the publisher is illegal and punishable by law. Please purchase only authorized electronic editions, and do not participate in or encourage electronic piracy of copyrighted materials. Your support of the author's rights is appreciated.

LIBRARY AND ARCHIVES CANADA CATALOGUING IN PUBLICATION
Banks, Christopher, 1970–, author
The cloud versus grand unification theory / Chris Banks.
Poems.
Issued in print and electronic formats.
ISBN 978-1-77041-368-9 (softcover)
ISBN 978-1-77305-082-9 (PDF); ISBN 978-1-77305-083-6 (ePub)
I. Title.
PS8553.A564C56 2017   C811'.6   C2017-903739-0
C2017-903740-4

Purchase the print edition and receive the eBook free!
For details, go to ecwpress.com/eBook.

Editor for the press: Michael Holmes / a misFit book
Book design: Rachel Ironstone
Cover images: fish © www.glofish.com

The publication of *The Cloud versus Grand Unification* has been generously supported by the Canada Council for the Arts, which last year invested $153 million to bring the arts to Canadians throughout the country, and by the Government of Canada through the Canada Book Fund. *Nous remercions le Conseil des arts du Canada de son soutien. L'an dernier, le Conseil a investi 153 millions de dollars pour mettre de l'art dans la vie des Canadiennes et des Canadiens de tout le pays. Ce livre est financé en partie par le gouvernement du Canada.* We also acknowledge the support of the Ontario Arts Council (OAC), an agency of the Government of Ontario, which last year funded 1,737 individual artists and 1,095 organizations in 223 communities across Ontario for a total of $52.1 million, and the contribution of the Government of Ontario through the Ontario Book Publishing Tax Credit and the Ontario Media Development Corporation.

Printed and bound by Coach House Printing in Canada   5 4 3 2 1

III. *Selfie with Ten Thousand Things*
    Trophy Case 39
    Almanac 40
    Selfie with Ten Thousand Things 41
    Orpheus at Ethel's Lounge 43
    The Waves 44
    Parallel Universes 45
    Replicas 46
    Higher Power 47
    Narrative versus Lyric 49
    White Mansion 50
    Trojan Horse 52

IV. *Finders Keepers*
    The Understudy 55
    Trasheteria 56
    RCA 57
    Finders Keepers 58
    Viral 59
    Playback 61
    Wordsworth versus the Cloud 63
    Tsunami 64
    Fossil 65
    Devotion 66
    The Green Light 68

Some see a lake of fire at the end of it,
Or heaven's guesswork, something always to be sketched in.

I see a sullen boy in a video arcade.
He's the only one there at this hour, shoulders slightly bent above a machine.
I see the pimples on his chin, the scuffed linoleum on the floor.

I like the close-up, the detail. I like the pointlessness of it,
And the way it hasn't imagined an ending to all this yet

— from Larry Levis's "Boy in Video Arcade"

I
ALL-NIGHT ARCADE

PROGRESS

Gene-targeting and molecular cloning. The shrine
of the genome has been broken into — GloFish
the colour of Skittles, or an Apple product line, happily
swim in aquariums. Insulin-producing bacteria
are grown in large fermentation tanks to provide
medicine for diabetics. Frankenfruit are popular
at Whole Foods. Grapples. Tangelos. Seedless
watermelons. We need to take bioengineering
between species to the next level. There are
glow-in-the-dark-cats, featherless chickens,
web-spinning goats, sudden death mosquitos,
super cows, Enviropigs, but why not gene-splice
chameleons with butterflies? Imagine summer fields
thick with fairy creatures changing colours. How
about lemon-scented honeybees? Flying iguanas?
Why not unicorns? Why stop there? Demand
Big Pharma give us an altruism patch, one to create
more empathy in politicians, say, or a nasal spray
to make children more resistant to fear-mongering
and body shaming. What about you? What would
you want if you could simply overhaul your genes
with a micro-injection? A Mensa level intelligence,
a cat's vision in the dark, a custom-built SPF 70
front-loaded into one's epidermis? In the future,
chromozones will be upgraded like cell phone plans.
This is what progress looks like. It's coming fast,
although time augments us all the more subtly.
The way a marriage translates a person. Or a year
writing a book you eventually throw away. Careless
days at university. A small room. Your first time

making love to someone else: a nosebleed and
shared laughter over it, then intimacy, tenderness
at another's touch. The imperfect perfect.

ALL-NIGHT ARCADE

I am playing Galaga in my imagination
in the last century where all around me
kids packed tighter than bees in a hive
labour to master rows of arcade games,
crowding to witness if anyone makes it
to a new level, beats an old high score,
wipes out an army of extraterrestrials.
Time and space stand still for the price
of a quarter. Pixellated blooms burst in
neon cascades across our beatific faces
while the world drags on into the ruins
of the '80s. Ronald Reagan is shot.
The great hurts and loves of this world
enter into us. Childhood one more urn
in History's mausoleum. Psychedelic Furs,
My Bloody Valentine, the Jesus and Mary
Chain. Mix-tapes for a generation who
witness the *Challenger* explode,
the Exxon Valdez spill, the Berlin Wall
topple with an empire. In our twenties,
the arcades vanish. The circumference
of the planet enlarges. We leave home
for school or to work jobs in big cities,
summers in Europe, but time is theft,
and we soon ascend to the next round,
a millennial collect-a-thon with all-new
obstacles to jump over, skill challenges
to undertake. More enemies, less lives.
Nostalgia is a verdict for not living well,
which is why in my forties all night long
I sit here watching myself as a teenager

play a video game with time running out,
a pilgrim trying to get to the golden city
at the last level, knowing when the game
is over, neither he nor I will continue.

CONFESSIONALISM

Ashbery is a bore. W. is a hack with a rhyming dictionary. M. is the best poet we have. I stole the milk money in grade three. Killed a grizzly bear with a Boy Scout knife. I have no idea how to wear my hair. I won the Boston Marathon. I can recite all of Vonnegut verbatim. Elegies are morose, but so are shopping malls. I am banned from Rome and Prague for life. The soul is a nice daydream. I once met with a university professor to talk poetry on LSD. My books are all ghostwritten by my twin. I am paranoid delusional, and believe a cabal of poets is out to get me. I won the lottery three times. I'd rather read the Brontë sisters than Dostoevsky six days out of a week. There should be a surcharge every time someone uses

the words "filigree" or "palimpsest" in a poem.
All my conquests are illegitimate. Barren trees,
huge uprooted lungs, standing amidst winter
fields, breathing cold air, are amongst my
favourite things. I love how you like this poem
despite its narcissism. I lived in a Buddhist
monastery for six whole months. I summited
Everest. There are women in this world who
harden when my name is mentioned. I was
pen pals with Jack Gilbert. Larry Levis too.
This has all happened to me. This is all true.

TRIGGER WARNINGS

A lightning strike kills three hundred reindeer in Norway. Bodies draped over a green mountain like an existential diorama. I'm calling my personal transformation a remix. Even when there is no path, there is a secret path, said my daughter, at age two. Marcus Aurelius wrote, "What stands in the way becomes the way." Well, my friends, sobriety is no yellow brick road. Live a good life. Do not hurt anyone. But something has to be the new dope, or it's back to the old neurotoxins. I have a disease of eternal longing. What if I want the leaves to change? To brighten, but not to fall? Like everyone, I hide insurance in a box, pass the hours with circuitry and tweets. I want to hoard the cosmos, not fears. Did you know an octopus has three hearts? Our sun will burn out in five billion years? Why is the Saviour always appearing on a potato chip, or a piece of toast, or in someone's dreams? Why not rematerialize on a talk show? Please, I need a remedy or a destination. An alphabet to reclaim. A personal continuity editor. Am I the hero or the villain? I wish I could just watch reruns, and be happy. My emotions glitch, and suddenly I need a reboot. The world is full of trigger warnings, and there I am pulling the triggers. Anxiety is walking down a sidewalk on a summer's day feeling caught in a giant centrifuge. It adds a dash of metaphysical clarity to life. It summons you, bones and flesh, to witness the sad strip malls, and nail salons sitting like jails on street corners. Either make peace with the heart hammering the bent nail of one's spirit, or not. Look again at those pictures of dead reindeer, and there in a corner, see your animal self among them.

THERE IS A LIGHT THAT NEVER GOES OUT

I hear that song "There Is a Light That Never Goes Out"
but it rings less true than it did once upon a time.
The older we get, the more we turn to silhouettes,

so when I hear the chorus, I feel only at a distance
from the telltale guitar of Johnny Marr or Morrissey's cries.
His voice singing, *there is a light that never goes out*,

a requiem to teenage years that never quite existed
except in old music videos or the pages of *Rolling Stone*.
No, the older we get, the more we turn to silhouettes

where our memories, mere shadows of sense, emerge
on the other side of a train platform in a black-and-white film
or like a sweeping beam of light that never goes out

cutting through a fogbank warning ships off rocks,
the shoreline obscured, invisible, too far away to imagine.
No, the older we get, the more we turn to silhouettes.

Our leather jackets with band patches and buttons
hang in the closet or attic. We raise our children
saying our love is a light that never goes out,
while slowly they watch us turn to silhouettes.

AMPLIFIER

Standing stoop-shouldered, coaxing power chords
from an electric guitar, a teen boy catapults sounds
out his bedroom window. The neighbourhood one big
amphitheatre. With each chord progression, the boy

drifts further away from anxiety and disillusionment.
Punk rock nothing more than Sturm und Drang angst
sprung from a Peavey amplifier. Its black matte box
a sonic blotter of everything he hates about existence.

His guitar's patch-cord umbilicus connects him in utero
to heroes like Kurt Cobain and J Mascis.
An imaginary world just as real and significant
as the one outside where the darkness comes on,

slowly filters through the trees in his backyard.
No one hears what he hears as he stands hunched over
his guitar, withdrawing into song and his own time,
the posters on his walls familiar companions,

his synapses kicked into overdrive, his veins thumping
with a finite earthly music he believes has the power
to smash the world and reassemble it into something
a teenager might finally understand. What is *this* anyway?

There is the ordinary and there is the sublime
although it will be years before he sees life in such terms,
yet both are conjoined in the buzz-feed he generates
from a little black box covered in a finely woven cloth.

THE HUNDREDS

Eight-tracks of Neil Diamond's *Hot August Night* are gone.
Cassettes lost. Don't look, but Betamax and VHS tapes
are no more. All around us, the old century, *The Hundreds*
as my daughter calls it, is vanishing. The K-car is gone.
Wood-panelled basements and macramé wall hangings.
Airbrushed vans, teen hitchhikers, Corvette summers.
Moon landings. Woodstocks. Live Aid. Lollapaloozas.
Henry Morgentaler and Ian Curtis are gone. Terry Fox
and Andy Kaufman. East Germany and Czechoslovakia.
The rotary phone is gone. The modem is gone. Even
intricately folded high-school notes, written in cursive
in April of 1986, no longer exist. The Khmer Rouge
and Nelson Mandela are gone. Kennedy and Brezhnev too.
Atari is gone. The arcades are gone. Pong. Pac-Man.
Donkey Kong. Transistor radios. Walkmans. Discmans.
Boomboxes. Ghetto blasters. Hi-fi stereo receivers.
Billie Holiday, Satchmo, John Lennon, Freddie Mercury.
Rock. New Wave. Punk. Hardcore. Grunge. Shoe-gaze.
I cannot tally it all, but still I keep trying like a man
poring over microfiche, not memories, hoping for a clue
or two that might tell a person how to live
with loss when already oceans are rising, the climate
is changing, the animals are leaving us, one species
at a time: *Dusky seaside sparrow. Mexican grizzly bear.
Golden toad.* The past seems more real than a world
where Greenland is melting, where people stare at phones
the way they once did at paintings. *The Hundreds*,
smelling of old money, sibling rivalry and white privilege
are not coming back, and it's time for time to settle up,
to explain what it was all about, before we too one day,
after breakfast, or a walk in the park, or a trip to the city,
find ourselves suddenly, and irrevocably, gone.

ROADSIDE ATTRACTIONS

Most poems I read feel like I'm walking through
someone's private zoo. One of those sad-looking
affairs with a hand-painted sign just off a highway
with a bear in a cage sitting with his back to you,
a fox obsessively pacing the perimeter of a fence.
Look, a bear, you say, and then you buy a pennant
at the souvenir shop doubling as a main office.
Most do not register a tremor on the Richter scale,
can't even make you feel the sky is actually blue,
so caught up as they are with being clever, not
that there are not some fine lines, but the scope
is always so small. A bouncy castle of metaphors.
In this time of mass extinctions and exorbitant
debt, what I want a poem to be is a kind of ark
to float above it all. Try to pack in the Eros and
the lightning, the thunder and the destruction,
the nuclear spillage, bad sex, pop music, sarin
gas, child soldiers. Fill it to overflowing with
nameless tropical storms, celebrity Chihuahuas,
corrupt bankers, SSRIs, third world carnage,
empty car washes, dynamite. Entitle it "Notes
Toward an Epic Poem." Surely we can live in
a perpetual great astonishment, as Roethke said,
or maybe I am just being clever. Maybe this is
another roadside attraction, a cabinet of curiosities,
and I'm filling it with whatever interests me,
smoky old movie theatres with radium clocks,
a postcard of Paris, dead flowers, tarnished keys.
Maybe I am the bear in the cage who does not
want to see the world the way it is, the steel bars,
the concrete floor. Exit through the gift shop.

EMPIRE OF TIME

Past the alpha and omega, past being and becoming, past the Monkees,
    past Walt Whitman and William Carlos Williams, past Al Purdy

and Gwendolyn MacEwen, past CBC and reruns of *The Edge of Night,*
    past Chilliwack and April Wine, past KISS and the Bay City Rollers,

past determined shoppers digging through racks at BiWay and Woolsworth,
    past Waco and Columbine, past Fat Man and Little Boy, past the alpha

and the omega; past Scout meetings in church basements, past teen
    dances in school gymnasiums, past the Vietnam War and draft dodgers

opening food co-ops in rural Ontario; past the October Crisis
    and the Squamish Five, past hippies and free love and DIY communes;

past the white noise of politics, past the eulogizing of prime ministers,
    past the holy scripture of *Mad* magazine, past the '80s and the Brat Pack;

past adolescence, its altar of self-loathing, past Iran-Contra and
    Chernobyl, past Cabbage Patch dolls and Rubik's Cubes and New Coke,

past virgin Redwood Forests and a plastic-free Sargasso Sea; past Glasnost
    and Perestroika, past free trade and a factory in every town, past

armies of unionized workers and Halley's Comet, the World Wide Web
    and Tiananmen Square; past poetry readings, obsessive addictions

to learning — the Cult of Illumination — past late night Montreal falafel shops
    and the beautiful girl you left crying at a deserted café in the rain; past

the Oklahoma City bombing, royal divorces, past the point of no
    return, past the Hubble Telescope and the Mars Pathfinder missions,

past neon signs and the grammar of despair; past the Large Hadron Collider
    and Y2K, past closed porno theatres and a corporate Times Square;

past 911 and a handgun in every drawer; past marriages and divorces,
    the secret lives of our neighbours, past children, past forever climbing

Jacob's corporate ladder, past lies and promises, past our own self-pity
    and skin wrinkles; past Occupy movements and Arab Springs, past

celebrity memoirs, past faith-science binaries, past planets circling
    a giant gigawatt nuclear sun, past the alpha and the omega.

COMMUNION

Yesterday, a stranger
    waved furiously at me
until as I drew closer

    he realized his mistake
disappearing down
    the road which left me

mulling over all day
    who he thought I might
have been, or if I am

    who I am, which is to say
are we anyone at all
    beyond a lingering shadow

hiding inside ourselves
    waiting for strangers to wave
so we might wave back.

REALITY CHECK

Checking *one, two, three*. Is this thing on?
Happenstance is my religion. All praise
the new economy. FoxConn manufactures
serfs and gizmos. The housing market is
a trap door waiting to open. Our gospel is
Spotify. Don't worry about those defunct
factories. Those brick buildings crumbling
in the downtown core. The rich will likely
convert them into luxury lofts, and get
a picture taken with the mayor. Win-win.
Except often we lose little bits of ourselves
in the process. No more strawberry socials
or neighbours sitting together on front
porches. Just the occasional road rage
and awkward queues in grocery-chain stores.
Strangers trying to quietly contain joy
and terror, madness from setting in, until cut
off suddenly at a red light, the limbic brain
goes full ape. Brouhahas occur. Trickle-
down economics has left us with dribbles.
Yes, I am leaving parts out of the frame.
What about the bird-watchers and book
clubs? The people multiplying happiness
like loaves and fishes? Cynicism is a type
of camera obscura. I admit it. Pardon me
for weighing vice over virtue, but I can't
help feeling like reality is a test of faith.
I choose life most days. Even with its
endless construction and Rx peddling,
its dinner time cold calls, its coughing fits,

its tax forms and online trolls. I wish
the human heart was appraised the way
diamonds are. A pound of flesh is worth
more than stone. Take that to the bank.

II
THE CLOUD VERSUS GRAND UNIFICATION THEORY

DUSK TILL DAWN

You imagine the moon filling a bedroom window
as the towering screen of a drive-in movie theatre
high above a winter field strewn with meltwater.
Soon cars prowl past the ticket booth's *closed* sign.
An unlighted snack bar hunched in snow and rain
gathers a crowd. The moth-stutter of faint images
flicker from a projector filled with stopped clocks.
Someone has already begun to lay aside his clothes
in a borrowed car. Someone's white bare shoulder
is sending a boy's desire up in flames, burning him.
Someone feels branded by delight. Even on a night
as cold, as ordinary as this evening, somewhere it is
the summer of 1985 and *Back to the Future* is playing.
Somewhere people stagger in between rows of cars,
drinking beer, laughing heartily, suspecting nobody
will ever grow old, or expire, or be forgotten again.
Many are wrong — it is already tomorrow's music
leaking out of FM radios, speaker poles like crosses
marking the graves of teens who came before them,
until someone finds himself locked out of some car,
twenty years older with an adolescent girl long dead
in a car wreck. What happened two decades ago.
Someone wishes he could go back to another time
to loiter under a different moon, in another century,
but already there is a fight in the parking lot. Already
police are gathering at the entrance, waiting for dawn
to come, for people to finally get tired and go home,
while someone drunk yells *Come on!,* holds up his fists
unaware the invisible projectionist who is smoking
absentmindedly, dusting ashes off one last cigarette,
stares out his tiny window, knowing how it all ends.

ENVOY AT THE CROSSROADS

Already we see the bush-party fires
when police stop the car and a cop
asks where we might be going. He
shines a flashlight in the windows
unable to detect the open bottles
at our feet. None of us can speak,
four boys joy-riding after midnight,
caught as we are in the past tense.
Across the creek, we hear laughter.
The shrieks of denim-clad nymphs
disappearing like smoke through trees
pursued by plaid-shirted farm boys
gone mad from loneliness, alcohol.
Where are you going? the cop repeats,
a little bored. How many times has
he asked this question to strangers
on a highway, caught between there
and here, an envoy at a crossroads,
staring evenly into eyes full of fear,
drunken rage? From my perspective
all I see is his flashlight. In a minute,
we will turn our car around to head
into the darkness. Fireworks explode
above the creek which go unnoticed
by the cop who is already fading into
shadow. Peonies, red, gold, shower
night skies, yet to see rockets bloom
is to forget this happened long ago

when we were young. What the past
extinguishes not even memory holds
together, which is why no one looks
in the rear-view to see the officer
standing at his post, guarding
our trespasses, the sky raining fire.

TEMPLE

Friday night dances at the Temple,
girls bangled in pink neon, lip gloss,
smoke machines and strobe lights,
some DJ hidden in a corner behind
turntables, triple-stacked speakers.
Frankie telling us all to just relax
while three boys are drinking gin
in a bathroom, trying to summon
up the courage to dance or fight.
These memories add up to nothing,
and yet the music is real. I live in
the Temple of my imagination, one
without an altar, but idols are many —
the English Beat is playing, and
Devo. Elvis Costello and the Clash.
The three boys have moved onto
the dance floor. Should I stay or
should I go?
                One might even be me,
but it is hard to tell from a distance,
what with all the smoke and lights
and intervening years. Still I watch
his movements as his body shuffles,
tries to follow where the beat leads,
the same way I follow these words,
stumble after rhythms of a language
I thought I learned at birth. The tempo
slows, so each boy stands with hands
in pockets, until a group of girls ask
them to dance, and the ritual begins.
The slow waltz toward the future.

LOST ACRES VARIETY

You cannot find it easily. Its storefront
        appears on dirt roads

on the other side of wood-covered bridges;
        or on highways bounded

by dark medieval woods, or rising
        from dredged timber pilings

in thick swamplands. Its leaded windows
        are covered in the faded ink

of newspapers centuries old. Sunshine
        has bleached its wooden sign,

letters missing. Its screen door hangs off
        rusty hinges, full of holes.

The little bell above the entranceway
        jangles in a cool breeze announcing

the arrival of spiders and yellow jackets;
        nothing else. The cash register

sits open full of old coupons, and leaves
        left to rot. Time circles slowly

here like the fan above its worn store shelves
        still stocked with those things

we shall need: *rain, shoelace, robin's egg,*
        meadow, spool, beach glass.

THE CLOUD VERSUS
GRAND UNIFICATION THEORY

I am not asking for anything except a little wisdom
from this life. Experience has taught me to be
prepared for when a bullet passes clean through,
it leaves a hole behind. Praising things is its own job.
That we might actually *know* two or three people,
despite battalions of online friends, is a consolation
prize for not solving the Grand Unification Theory
or writing thirty novels or discovering a ninth planet.
Living becomes its own masterpiece. A catalogue
of blunders and missteps and then, a surprise party!
I have met a few certifiable geniuses in my day
and they were all disappointingly human. Failure
is a bogeyman. What happens next is up to you.
The brain does not care we are only so many miles
of nerve-endings. It wants to go further off-leash.
What is the real story here? Some days, it is all
caviar and champagne, and the next, forty horses
die in a barn fire. No angels earn their wings. People
lie to each other out of fear, to spare each other's
feelings. What kind of man does that make me?
I tell elaborate lies to ascertain the truth. I resolve
to get out of bed most mornings, to witness
the past like a boarded-up pawn shop, to read
what life throws in my path the way ancient priests
read bones, which is to say inscrutably. Make it
up anyways. What I need is another mass grave
for my doubts to pile into. I keep thinking about
that engineering student who tied a piece of rope
to a hydro pole, passed it through his car's window,
before cinching it around his neck and driving off,

or a woman I saw once spread her arms before
diving off a three-storey parking lot. At what
point do we give up and surrender to our desires,
even if they end up killing us? Maybe I'm being
greedy wanting art to be more than a bowl of fruit,
wanting there to be answers. Who is listening?
The partygoers nibble the caviar and move on.

PANIC ROOM

It is seven in the morning and I can see the couple
    next door heading to work. People pull coats
around themselves, scrape frost from windshields. No
    one acknowledges anyone else, which makes it
hard to believe people are still making love, but I know
    they are, for their children are heading to school too.
Perhaps it is like Chekhov said. When you are in love,
    it shows a person who he should be. But this world's
day-to-day living makes mockery of such vulnerabilities
    so we stuff emotions with self-loathing, gastro pubs,
online shopping, pharmaceuticals, alcohol, social media,
    anything, really, so as not to feel human and alive. The
weather, of course, is not helping. The cold winter air
    steals our breath so we seal ourselves deeper in a living
slowly wearing people out. No one likes to talk about it,
    especially in poetry. Write about childhood or politics,
your dog or your ex, but not about the invisible fires
    of existence. When asked why he always wore black,
Chekhov said he was mourning his life. How many
    deny doing this? We watch cat videos and zombies
on television, or rail about the latest national scandal
    meant to keep us preoccupied and not thinking about
the world's clock near midnight. A sliver of moon
    hangs like a silver scar in the morning sky. I can only
drink so much coffee before admitting I am trying
    to avoid panic attacks through apathy. Somewhere,
my children are smiling, going to school blissfully
    unaware of consciousness's cold depths. What to do
with such thoughts? In California, a lake has fallen
    off a cliff, and still there are droughts. The Philippines

is sinking. I ask myself, *What am I going to do today?*

The answer is always the same: something is not right. Time is out of joint so Prince Hamlet keeps cursing

his wretched spoiled existence, while twenty years on, I keep trying to celebrate all the varieties of experience

through a few words that will break the wall grown up between the subjective and the objective, the self

and the other. I keep looking for release. The angels in the high cradle we built for them mock me. So be it.

Maybe all we are is random acts of kindness between strangers. Maybe it is my job to hear the pain singing

in every particle of my flesh. Maybe it means nothing. I have probably said too much. Certainly the couple

who smile at me when we chance meet at the mailbox are not thinking about any of this. They are thinking

about their ten-year anniversary and novelty lingerie and perhaps what wine to pair with tonight's dinner.

Soon I will rouse myself, throw on clothes, then write this all down. It will sound vaguely like a panic room.

Like I have built a secret place out of my fears and joys to linger in awhile, biding what is left of my time until

you who happen by, hearing me, throw open a door.

ALCOHOL

That deep dark woods.

That troll under the bridge.

That suicide bomber in Toys Я Us.

That Bermuda Triangle. That hopeless flirt.

That one-man zombie apocalypse.

That singalong in Hell. That plastic church.

That monster in the labyrinth.

Half-man. Half-beast.

Still thirsty.

JUKEBOX OF NOCTURNES

Choose your paradigm shift. An old girlfriend dies and all I think of is the outline my body makes as it passes through the air. Sometimes I want to wake free of thoughts, which would be its own kind of death. Getting older is like watching a blizzard sneak up on a small city. The tribulations of the ordinary still leave one scared. What are the set coordinates, you may ask, for happiness? I never see myself as part of the overall composition. Climate change is hysterical. Imagination is a scout at the edge of the frontier. If you forget that, then you deserve your unalloyed clarity. I walk through my day, and the world reflects me in a puddle, a store window, a watch face. It gets to a point where I have to ignore shadows. Nostalgia immolates the heart. Time is a marquee sign missing letters. A jukebox full of nocturnes. Most days I am trying to translate the word *emblem* into something I can touch and feel. To say anything new is a fable. Read those gilded pages. Inspiration calls back. Do you want the truth or its placebo? Let us build a lifetime together. You go first. Love is its own reproof against darkness. A pyre of joy. The tiny voice in your head says I am right.

SEPARATION

After coming early to walk along the beach
I can see all the way across Georgian Bay:
the flannel of clouds in faint haze, and
the island looming in the middle distance.
Standing in wet sand, I watch angry gulls
starting turf wars, the island barely visible
through the wind blowing cold off the lake,
bringing with it voices of Huron and Petun,
tribes who spent a hard winter on that rock
and starved to death in 1649. Belief a tether
held them together just long enough to die.
Huge white burls of whitecaps are rolling in,
searching for bodies to inhabit. An old couple
pick their way across the sand with tiny dogs
ignoring the man at the water's edge. I look
out at the island knowing it stares back at me
uncomprehendingly, not seeing me out here
in the open, detached from everything, one
with so little to hold onto, for nobody inherits
the earth. Bones of the Huron and the Petun
tell us salvation comes too late. On the horizon,
the island floats at the farthest edges of sight,
a distant place no one may reach. A sanctuary
to those long forgotten tribes who tried to live
eternally behind walls of faith that fell apart
making it clear: if you are waiting for someone
to rescue you, start with yourself, or all is lost.

HOW IT WORKS

The city looks bombed out. Huge holes
hidden behind wooden barriers. Craters
excavated. Traffic snarled for months.
Orange-clad work crews fit rebar, pour
cement. A concrete burrow emerges.
A parking garage. Glass condominiums
arise where a brick building once stood.
Construction is ongoing. People pass
beneath cranes expecting a piano to fall
on their heads. Meanwhile new detective
shows appear on television. New apps
occupy the children. All coffee shops
advertise free wireless, but the patrons
sitting at tables, not speaking, appear
full of invisible wires. Sometimes
a person raises his head, looks outside
to the plywood barriers staple-gunned
with flyers, playbills. He complains
about gentrification. The way it used
to be. There are interventions occurring
in the suburbs, where fentanyl
has taken hold of a son or a daughter
and yet downtown, a woman wearing
yoga pants reads a poem on a patio
about da Vinci's *Vitruvian Man*. There
a young couple is laughing, a first date,
talking about the fabulous sandwiches
at a local bakery, an online Kickstarter,
a bike-sharing program, when suddenly
it strikes you: the cranes, the barriers,

the pits each rush hour crawls around,
this city is being rebuilt for them, not
you, which is when you hear it, a siren
speeding toward the scene of a crime.

VENTRILOQUISM

I've learned to throw my voice. I started small
by mimicking the sound of a breeze in shrubs,
a dog on a chain behind a wooden fence, kids
playing touch football in the street, but I have
grown more confident. Now nothing appears
too ambitious for my stagecraft. The silence
grown up between two people whose marriage
is an elaborate exercise in taxidermy. Panic
after a nightclub shooting. A woman angry
in an upper-storey apartment window, clothes
raining down onto a man who lowers his head
on the sidewalk, saying, "I'm sorry for this . . ."
to every passerby. The hum of street lights
bathing the homeless. The sighs of the alkies
approaching last call, oblivion. The terrible
cleaving when, at thirteen, the world divides
into good and evil. The little boy banging on
the nailed-shut windows of the last century.
The blitzkrieg of corporations offering poison,
prescription drugs to the suburbs. The thing is
I have become so good at it, merging my voice
with warfare and politics and memes, I am not
sure what I sound like anymore. The world gets
lost in the delivery. It's confusing. My lips are
sealed. Hear that calling? I counterfeit well.

III
SELFIE WITH TEN THOUSAND THINGS

TROPHY CASE

The last passenger pigeon, Martha,
dies in the Cincinnati Zoo in 1914
as Europe sinks like a mastodon
beneath the mud of battlefields.
What does it feel like not to exist?
I've been alive forty years, and will
never see a black carpet of birds
a mile wide, thirty miles in length,
pass over Southwestern Ontario.
An avian eclipse. *Evening all afternoon*
as Mr. Stevens says. I picture huge
migrating flocks, great phalanxes.
A cathedral of wings flying high over
big cities and towns. Dark miracles.
Who would believe such things today?
Audubon writes of a swarm so large
it takes days to pass over his head.
I keep thinking of little Martha asleep
in a museum, America's trophy case,
dreaming of extinction, while families
go to church Sundays, sing hymns,
pray to be taken away. I am afraid
of a world where I may cease to be,
which is why I imagine a green hill,
a storm of pigeons passing overhead,
myself a witness to a heavenly host.

ALMANAC

Driving I see bus shelters for school kids,
tiny gabled huts standing by the highway,
cold-war era gatehouses, all checkpoints
leading to a country beyond this country
where farmer's almanacs predict weather
and the elm trees go on dying each year
beside one-room schoolhouses. Little boys
and girls dressed like miniature adults
sell maple syrup at roadside fruit stands.
Horses and buggies shoulder the highway.
Broken-ribbed barns fall apart near steel
blue historical signs and fieldstone walls.
This is the Kingdom of the Way It Was.
An unreal country of thumb-worn bibles
in bedside tables. Of grandfather clocks
swinging giant pendulums till doomsday.
A border crossing between yesterday
and tomorrow. Everything feels yoked
to appearances. I wish I knew another
way of seeing and living in the world.
A tire-swing hangs in a yard. The future
is impenetrable. Takes a rain check.
A young Mennonite man in a black cap
rides a bicycle toward a coming storm,
a prisoner sentenced to life who knows,
staring at the fields, none of us are free.

SELFIE WITH TEN THOUSAND THINGS

One monarch butterfly is worth a hundred sonnets.
    Hazlitt didn't say that, I did, in the middle of my life,
concerned less with fugues and arias, picaresques or
    Bildungsromans. Now I think more about old-timers,
the kind who at AA meetings say, "I was sick and tired
    of being sick and tired." The marrow of the sentiment
sadly the closest thing to truth in my life. Maybe it is
    an illusion any of us are alive. It is impossible to

say just what I mean, and even then, I did not say
    those words, Eliot did, a hundred years ago. Think
of this poem as my coming out as a great pretender.
    Think of it as a selfie with ten thousand things.
What do you think? Really, that is all that should matter
    when we turn on our televisions to learn another
landslide has swept a village off the face of the earth,
    or a rogue coyote has claimed an old lady's cat, or

a fatwa has been dealt to another foreign journalist.
    No one has ever told you this, but the self, the soul,
burns brightest with a bomb strapped to its back —
    illness, say, or a doomed relationship. Alcoholism.
The hell we made. I try not to think about death,
    but most hours it is singing at the top of its lungs
in the hallway outside my door. A bad neighbour.
    What is truth one minute is simply lies the next.

The gods do not talk of men anymore. I fall asleep
    thinking of James Wright and horses. Soft muzzles.
The sweetest grass still on the other side of the fence.
    Everything these days can be found on the internet,

but I want new knowledge: no more light or flowers,
    something I can be faithful to, the brick and mortar
of another life, which if it were not for me, somebody
    else would, out of habit, set accidentally on fire.

ORPHEUS AT ETHEL'S LOUNGE

We hadn't seen him in several weeks
until there he was, alone on a bar stool,
looking thinner, paler, sipping whiskey.
He ignored the regulars playing pool,

the jukebox country music. His lyre
was missing. The next stool sat empty.
When asked what happened to what's-her-name,
his shoulders sank. His faith expired.

I turned my back, he said, wiping his eyes.
A few drunks nodded, saying they understood.
The bartender brought him another rye.
It was clear she was gone for good.

It was written on his face. A haunted look
leading down to a bottomless place.

THE WAVES

On the beach, my daughter fills a void,
holding sand in one hand, letting it out a little
at a time, taking it apart, adding it up. She builds
a sandcastle with dirty fingers to be an object,
a core sample of the real and the measurable,
while my son wrings the air in his fierce joy,
gull-stepping, like a baby-king, into the surf;
white crests lap against his pudgy knees.
Each time he walks out, turns, comes in again,
the whole of what he is gathers in rhythm
with the water's rush and ebb against the shore;
his body is pure tumult, as he claps his hands
going out farther each time, his motion the wave
his sister recognizes, rushes out to greet.

PARALLEL UNIVERSES

They exist, scientists say. Schrödinger's cat,
both alive and dead, inhabits the same box
in a multiverse where all possible histories,
futures are happening. In another dimension,
you are happy at your dream job. The family
doesn't break up. You win the award. No one
wants for love or money. It is like this poem:
quantum entanglement, subatomic particles
in two places, at once, says simultaneously
you are reading this, but also trying to recall
years later, a poem you read about parallel
universes. The poet forgotten. The details
obscured, yet steeped in new significance
because a poem feels more real than life,
at times. Maybe you meet someone who
looks like you, a doppelgänger. Or you
find yourself haunted by thoughts you left
unspoken, actions you did not undertake.
You are worried about choices you made.
Quantum mechanics provides another
library of possibilities: you moved back to
Montreal. You went to law school. You
never wrote a single poem ever. Truth
is irrelevant when science says it is all
happening. Cancer is cured. Wars end.
The dead are alive. You are here.

REPLICAS

A man in Kentucky builds a model of Noah's ark
for $100 million dollars. Designer handbags, shoes,
perfumes may be purchased in underground malls
for a tenth of the price. Max Ernst or Wolfgang
Beltracchi? The art world keeps burning catalogues.
Nietzsche statuettes, mustachioed, wearing a crown
of thorns, or a Justin Bieber poster, chest spritzed,
glowing with self-adulation. Ancient Thera is gaining
popularity with cruise ships. Civil war battles are
a form of entertainment. Lap dancers wear nudity
like a glorified costume. Authenticity requires time
most people would rather spend at Walmart. A map
is not the places within it. A picture of a sunset is not
the same as the world turning dark. The past is damaged
with each memory. I try to concern myself with big
thoughts, climate change, dark matter, mimetics, but
it is the other ones — eat, sleep, reproduce — which are
the human story repeating itself to itself. A lullaby
echoing back to an invisible source. Natural flavour
trumps nature every time. I want to caress the real,
and hold it tight. Life is an allegory of the blood.
If you want to live, you have to be more than
a cheap imitation or a brand. I read a lot of novels
and go to sleep alone. I avoid wax museums.
I remember MacEwen saying poets are magicians
without quick wrists. I hear despair in that statement
for the first time. I drag my ruined self from year
to year, worry I am an imposter. Someone builds
a giant transforming robot in a junkyard. A garish
copy of Versailles. They appear happy.

HIGHER POWER

I would rather talk about the elephant
in the room I must always keep with me,
who likes to drink alone and stare into
mirrors and squeezes me so tight some
nights I think I may burst from my skin
than you who are only so much bad fog
on another dull morning drive to work.
You who exist only in the white spaces
of the page. Life is fleeting. Bad things
happen. An uncle gets cancer. The dog
has a stroke. A child dies. A hurricane
kills hundreds on some tropical island.
With your beard and vaulted darkness,
you sit back and watch it all happen.
A favourite TV show. Forget to check
your voice mailbox with its billions of
messages unanswered. I know it sounds
terrible, but I am just not that into you.
The elephant says you are a narcissist,
and that I am co-dependent. He says
I should have stopped seeing you ages
ago. Maybe things could have been
different. Cue the violins. I do admit
the world is exquisitely made, and still
it is flawed. I would like to tell you
a parable. There was a man who left
his father's house. The elephant says
to make up the rest. Can I ask one
question? Why tease us down here?
Just when things become so terrible
and unrelenting and dismal the sun

shines, a bird sings, my children smile
and it is like a whole orchestra has
started playing, in stereo, for me. Why
do that? Give us a taste of miracles?
The elephant says I should go down
to the graveyard, ask about heaven,
but I am too full of love right now,
and besides, I have your attention.

NARRATIVE VERSUS LYRIC

A narrative poem leaves a trail of crumbs
in a fairy tale. A lyric poem introduces
a swan, its neck bowed low, feather-soft,
to eat them. A narrative poem jumps
out of a burning building. A lyric poem
watches the blaze celebrate wood, mortar,
clay. A narrative poem takes no prisoners.
A lyric poem says the only prison is longing.
A narrative poem wants to talk about high
school, children playing tag, an argument
last night, old family stories. A lyric poem
wants to sit around obsessing about figs,
twilight, perfume. A narrative poem and
a lyric poem walk in to a bar. The narrative
poem asks for a beer. The lyric poem wants
something to make the light speak. The
narrative poem hates the lyric poem when
it talks like this. Its aura of pretentiousness.
The lyric poem keeps smiling, scribbling
a ghazal about flowers and mortality. When
the night is over, the drunk narrative poem
admits the lyric poem's flowers are lovely.
The lyric poem says it has always secretly
loved the narrative poem's honesty. They
fall into each other's arms. A child is born.

WHITE MANSION

A confederacy of suicides. Borowski died
breathing gas, head in an oven, twelve years
before Plath did the same trick. Paul Celan
drowned himself. John Berryman jumped
from a bridge. Pavese downed a handful of
barbiturates in a hotel room. Anne Sexton
poured herself a vodka martini and started
her car in a closed garage. Brautigan and
Mayakovsky died of self-inflicted gunshot
wounds. On and on it goes, a pageant of
death and despair, anxiety and suffering.
The mind can be like the wind, invisible
and everywhere, or it can be a goldfish,
a prize for some child who tossed a ball
into a small round bowl. Something to be
left upon a shelf and forgotten. Vanity
and obstinateness make for great poems,
but few friends. When the end came for
them, the silence must have felt like one
last round of applause. I often wonder
if it was poetry, learning the vocabulary
of what it means to be truly sentient, that
led to their suffering, or was it the thing
that kept them alive all those years before
they loaded the gun, or flicked on the gas,
or strolled toward the bridge. Lovers
abandon us. Damage is done. The work
always more than we are willing to give.
I want to smuggle some kindnesses into
these rooms of sorrows. Turn the pages
on these dead ones. Think about the girl

just sixteen, discovering her own poetry,
writing in a journal. There are birds and
clouds and a large white mansion sitting
atop a hill. She smiles unlocking the gates.

TROJAN HORSE

Consciousness is an elevator,
a chameleon's dream, cognition
shot from a neural cannon,
a top-secret containment unit,
an antediluvian calculator,
a pirate radio station, a newsfeed,
a magnifying lens, a multiplex,
an intruder in the control room,
a cheap knock-off, a universal
adaptor, an early warning system,
the soul's GPS, a hot mic,
a tiger hidden behind a false wall,
an underground war, a pulpy
tell-all, a monster in a closet,
a recording at the bottom of a well,
an impersonator, a message slowly
revealing itself in tea leaves,
a Trojan Horse lurking in the code,
sensory enjambment, a little
pink cloud, a metaphysical bloom,
a spiritual fetish.

IV
FINDERS KEEPERS

THE UNDERSTUDY

My understudy has been waiting in the wings,
making notes about my likes and my dislikes,
trying not to see things as they are, but as I
see them. He follows me to work and back
home again, considers my faults, my evasions,
what is left unsaid in the narrative of my life.
He considers the measures of my experience,
the quiet rage I feel looking at a patch of snow
while flipping through my bills at a mailbox,
my fear there is no such thing as a definite life
unconstructed, that beyond my boredom
and my pain, there is nothing more to be revealed.
He observes my temptations, my ambitions,
trying to make sense of the part he is to play,
which is difficult, as some acts have not yet
been written, so he must imagine possibilities
for a future only now taking shape. I feel
his presence, as I walk through my neighbourhood,
mimicking me, paying attention to the trees
as much as my thoughts, my understanding
that the past is a matter of distances
and yet within imagination's reach. He spends nights
trying to read what has become illegible. He waits
to take the stage of a slowly turning globe
knowing his time is imminent. That the actor
grows older, that change is renewal,
and that as I begin to forget my lines,
he is always there to remind me, to take over
if necessary. The performance will not be lost.
Only the lead will be recast. Not the role. It carries on.

TRASHETERIA

More cave than club. Cam, the Goth guy
who we thought was a snob, could be
found dancing alone to Alien Sex Fiend
while people saddled up to the bar, drank
Jägermeisters and Black Label beer.
All of us were young, dressed in black,
wearing combat boots like a uniform,
in love with a dive bar smelling of piss,
disinfectant. It is gone, of course,
become another bar, but I can go back
to it when I daydream. Those nights
we would say unbelievable things
to each other: Pete Murphy is god.
Punk is dead. Stanislavski and Andy
Warhol are overrated. I am in love
with those young people who were so
fearless in their opinions, and yet
secretly knew deep within their cells,
their bodies were hurtling forward
through time so they should order
one more round. We tried on selves
and when they did not fit, we tried on
each other. The years obliterate
certain moments, while others seem
to stay like this one. Bauhaus or
Tones on Tail are playing, and there
is Mel with her shy little girl smile
telling everyone to get up and dance,
the music loud and calling out.

RCA

My ex-wife's great-grandfather spent thirty years
inside a factory, hand-polishing wooden cabinets
for RCA Victor after train-hopping across Canada
to British Columbia where he lopped off treetops
with nothing more than a handsaw for two years.
It was the most dangerous job he could find offering
the most pay. He worked the many lumber camps,
saving money to bring his family all the way over
from Hungary. During the Depression, he stood
behind the chain-link fences among the whoops,
the shouts, the troops of men looking for work,
pointing only to his callouses, as if they testified
to a man's ability to swing a hammer all day long.
That is what salvation looks like to an ordinary man
whose curses were left behind in another country,
along with poverty, cousins, wars, social unrest.
What it takes to be happy is a willingness to work
ten hours a day, for a lifetime, doing nothing
as important as polishing light mahogany cases,
later Bakelite ones, until they gleam like minted
pennies, so your family may grow to thrive
on a small Montreal street like any other.
All those years coming home from the factories
smelling of beeswax and linseed oil, hanging
up a coat in a kitchen, sitting down to a meal
of thick savoury soup, were worth it, a small price
if his son could study drafting nights, as he did
during the war. A gift of no small magnitude,
which I gather is what makes a man each shift
place a cloth in hand, and with clear practice,
polish a music box, until like some masterpiece,
he hears the overture of his own triumph.

FINDERS KEEPERS

As Heraclitus put it, "we are and we are not."
It makes me think of kids playing video games.
How they are not the machines, but the ghosts
inside them. I feel like I'm sinking through time,
a wasp sinking in amber, yet nothing of me will
remain. "To Thine Own Self Be True" is a T-shirt,
or a bumper sticker at best. Perceptions, words
complicate experience. Tiny parcels of language
tied up in thoughts. YouTube is sexier. Portrait
of the Artist as Internet Sensation. Think web hits.
Not poems. If I had a billion dollars, I would still
be in debt to old masters. These lines are a test.
I want to be emancipated from my singular flesh.
Everything becomes a metaphor if you wait long
enough. The chasm between what you say and
what you mean is real. The bridge is not. Which
side are you on? Art is the wound. Not the healing.
What does a rowboat on a salt plain say about
how we live? Poetry knows but won't tell anyone.
Finders keepers. It is not what you see, but what
you perceive. Memory after a certain age comes
with spoilers. It is hard to keep the world together
through paradox, by thinking and feeling alone. Ask
questions to the darkness, and a voice will speak
back. Whose voice? Well, go ask the magnolia
why it blooms. See what I did there? Indirection
or derangement. That is where to find beauty,
the authentic, hosannas of form and expression,
the unlike joined together. Hunger at our core.

VIRAL

The Roman Empire conquered much
of the world not because their armies
were better at killing other armies, but
because their civil engineers built roads.
Someone invents electric light in 1800,
so our planet now resembles a gigantic
Lite-Brite chandelier hanging in space.
Wordsworth went slumming in Paris
during the French Revolution so later
undergraduates might muddle through
the *Prelude*. Newton's apple. Fibonacci's
zero. What is it to be human? Turn on
a smart phone. Loss goes viral despite
our best attempts to immunize ourselves
with antidepressants and room service.
I am tired of the deification of billionaires
who started businesses from a garage.
We should be paying attention to anyone
trying to save the whales or languages
thousands of years old from dying out.
Persons without nameplates stamped on
buildings or Michelin stars. Just decent
ordinary folks who know one day we will
be reduced to a litter of ashes, so they
spend time building machines to allow
deaf children to hear mothers. Villages
to have fresh water. Those with vision
who clean up our bloody messes, while
the rest of us worry about 401ks. Watch
anonymous strangers dance awkwardly

to pop music. Dear Universe, no more
candy or flowers. What is the big idea?
That sweetness in you starts talking to
a sweetness in me. We infect each other.

PLAYBACK

I've been thinking too much again
about the kid in the basement up
past his bedtime, recording songs
off the radio on a cassette recorder.
Memory is a mix-tape. Hit playback.
We write our life stories like song
lyrics on album sleeves. Lift a rock
to find a sword and sandals hidden
beneath it. Tie a thread to a doorway
so you may find your way out again.
Myths are self-help guides. Music is
magical thinking. No wonder teens
drown themselves in songs. Parents
hover over them like glass-bottomed
boats. When I was thirteen, songs
came from distant galaxies. Melody
the message. I wound and rewound
tapes, trying desperately to preserve
how they made me feel. Kids today
step into a stream. Stay submerged.
Is it possible life was more real then
than now? I made you this mix-tape.
It is a grainy home recording of '80s
electronica, dead pets, '90s grunge,
tattered notebooks, aughts singer-
songwriter introspections, weddings,
a few smuggled demos of the current
decade's deep cuts, divorces, except
that boy who is still in the basement
waiting for the one song to come on

the radio, one that will save his life,
cannot hear it, even though listening
in the dark is all he ever seems to do.

WORDSWORTH VERSUS THE CLOUD

I wandered lonely in the Cloud
looking for any traces of the life
I had once known. A real place
with a swing set in a field, sandlot
ball games, fist fights, forests
full of hidden forts. Train tracks
made flattened pennies. Clouds
synced only rain. Time circled
on wrists. Mothers called to children
from porches after ripening dusk
settled on freshly mown lawns.
No daffodils, but neighbourhood
gardens abounded. Clotheslines
connected backyards. The years
pegged out like laundry. It is possible
to return, at times, to follow again
the hockey-card clicking of a bike's
spokes down the brain's back alleys,
but it means withdrawing a little
from the digital onslaught —
the tabloid headlines, exclusive
offers, hate speech, click-bait, online
dating, free porn — that dissolves
the soul, and fills the heart
with a moribund indifference. How
many likes will this poem get? The
Cloud begins to filter the question
when in the distance, cap-guns
announce a war starting to rage.

TSUNAMI

A Japanese motorcycle dredged onto the shore,
marooned on a remote beach of British Columbia,
reveals the ocean has no ending and no beginning.
Its resurrection, second coming, is hard evidence

of shadow addresses. Things imagination fathoms.
A reminder how the everyday needs vandalizing.
Images arise, accrue on the flip side of perception,
words flash mob, the choreography unrehearsed,

energies gather, find release. The electrical effect
stun-guns our ennui, defibrillates natural objects
so invention comes to life. It begins with anything
wearing a halo of truth: a blow-up doll in a tree.

A gathering storm or a lantern in a battened cellar.
Surprise can be counted on to rise to the surface
like a Japanese Harley. That spook of recognition,
an invisible highway to ride on through our losses.

FOSSIL

To match in words
the impression
some extinct creature
left in mud long ago —
to be that permanent,
and still not there.

DEVOTION

Why does poetry have to be so damn personal
all of the time? Why can't I write a poem called
"Surveilling the Underworld" about a dead boy
who walks the banks of the River Styx looking
for his lost dog, a man holding his dead wife's
dress in his arms, four men in a floating raft
adrift for three days after their merchant ship
was sunk by a German U-boat? Why not write
a poem about devotion, a man's obsession with
stiletto heels, a woman's loyalty to a hairdresser,
the right shade of lipstick, a child's fear of God
and nightly prayers? An addict's choice of jail
over a twelve-step program, the only place they
can get clean? Darlings, everyone has that one
piece of clothing they will never throw away,
that one book they continually read every ten
years. Some people are as committed to pain
as others are to happiness. If someone were
to ask me what I am devoted to, I would say
the body. It is the one thing that won't let go
of me. Sorry, I am being personal again when
really I wanted to write something only for you,
my faithful reader, who I still believe in, who
puts up with my many asides and silly detours,
who assumes these lines are leading to a place,
if only I knew where, of understanding, which
is all anyone wants, really, a little understanding
to form allegiances to, and perhaps build upon,
despite solid dedications to lovers who worship
or neglect us, to our jobs stealing time better

spent with family and friends, our adherence to a particular brand of cologne or soda pop. Our fondness for first editions, or vintage pornography, or fly-fishing. Our admiration for a major league sports team, or morning donut with our coffee. Devotion is the coin of the realm and the currency of the heart. Everything else just pays the balance owing.

THE GREEN LIGHT

I still believe in it, the way I believe in love after divorce, Greek sunsets dropping orange-crimson fire over the Mediterranean Sea, or Cézanne's apples. Aromas of homemade soup. The smell of bookstores. Accordian-shimmers of moonlight over a black lake. I believe in it, a green light on a dock, Gatsby with his arms outstretched, as if he could catch all of history, all of time, or even just one girl he loved once in such an embrace. But to my high-school self it represented even more: a pathway, a door opening onto the imagination. An in-dwelling need to connect with *another world which is this one*, or so said Paul Éluard. The rabbit hole of metaphysics suddenly large and inviting, peeling away the camouflage of the quotidian so wonder could be released like a long held breath. I believe in the omniscience of rock lyrics, the criminal joy of jaywalking, singing badly and out of tune. I believe in reaching hands out to the day's unrealized possibilities even when the barbarians are at the city gates and the world is burning. Burning, or in ruins, women and children crying. I still believe in it, that vision of a solitary figure staring out over a darkened bay, lonely and a little afraid that what is sought is illusory, money, fame, love, trembling so unlike a human being, the boats hidden in the dark, the green light beckoning.

ACKNOWLEDGEMENTS

I would like to thank Chris Hutchinson, Autumn Getty, Jim Johnstone, Rob Taylor and Paul Vermeersch, who were the first readers of these poems. I would also like to thank Michael Holmes for his editing expertise, Emily Schultz for a top-notch copy-edit, and everyone at ECW Press. Poems from this manuscript first appeared in a chapbook, *Invaders* from Anstruther Press (2015), and in the magazines *Grain* and *Prism International*.

ABOUT THE AUTHOR

Chris Banks is the author of three previous collections of poems: *Bonfires, The Cold Panes of Surfaces,* and *Winter Cranes.* His first full-length collection, *Bonfires,* was awarded the Jack Chalmers Award for poetry by the Canadian Authors' Association in 2004. *Bonfires* was also a finalist for the Gerald Lampert Award for best first book of poetry in Canada. His poetry has appeared in the *New Quarterly, Arc Magazine,* the *Antigonish Review, Event,* the *Malahat Review,* and *Prism International,* among other publications. He lives and writes in Waterloo, Ontario.